PROPHETS & *Prophecy*

The Ministry of Prophets in the New Testament Church

WORKBOOK

**Includes Instructions For "Certificate of Mastery"
With The PDM Network**

WILLIAM EMMONS

Copyright © 2016 PDM PUBLICATIONS

PROPHETS & PROPHECY

Printed in the USA

ISBN: 978-0-9961701-3-0

Prepared for publication by: www.palmtreeproductions.com

. . . .

To contact the author:

www.pdministry.org

. . . .

INTRODUCTION

Prophet Bill Emmons has been an educator and a certified teacher with New York State since 1976. He was a mentor teacher and a department head in many of the schools where he taught. Beyond that, God called him to five-fold ministry as both a prophet, a teacher and a pastor. These things more than qualified him to write "Prophets & Prophecy", and to create this companion workbook. Prophet Emmons has in essence created a balanced, Bible centered college level course on prophets, prophetic ministry, the proper use and development of spiritual gifts in the Church.

The workbook you hold in your hand has been designed to help you get the most from the "Prophets & Prophecy" book. The author's hope is to focus your attention on the information that he believes is of vital importance, and to check your understanding of what you should have learned in reading his book. As you go through this workbook please keep in mind that successfully completing each chapter <u>DOES NOT</u> qualify you as a prophet, nor does it confirm your area of ministry. What it does do is allow you to better understand the ministry and function of prophets in the New Testament Church. You will discover how the different prophetic levels operate and how the different kinds of prophets and prophetic meetings fit into God's design for His Church.

For the honest student of God's word, the book and workbook, or the entire course will bring tremendous clarity. For every congregation member it will bring increased understanding for where and how they fit into the local church. For those called to five-fold ministry, it will help define and develop how the prophetic realm flows together with what God may have called them to do in His Kingdom.

Each chapter in this workbook corresponds to the same chapter in the book "Prophets & Prophecy". You should read one chapter of the book and then do the corresponding workbook chapter. Do as much of it as you can from memory and then use the book to confirm or complete your answers as needed. The assigned point values for each question are in brackets, to the left. These values are used by the PDM Network for those taking the PDM "Prophets & Prophecy" course. A passing score of 90% or above on each chapter is needed to issued a final exam and provide a "*Certificate of Mastery*" for the PDM course students.

May God enrich you and cause you to grow strong as you study His word, read over the "Prophets & Prophecy" book and do this companion workbook.

May God Bless You In Your Studies.

Prophet William Emmons

OUR CONTACT INFORMATION

When contacting PDM please indicate if it is regarding the PDM Network, the "Prophets & Prophecy" book, workbook, college course with "Certificate Of Mastery", or to schedule an "on sight" teaching of the Prophets & Prophecy course. You may also make a request for Prophets Bill and Esther Emmons to come minister at your location.

Email

PropheticDestinyMinistry@gmail.com
wemmons@gmail.com

Regular Mail

Prophetic Destiny Ministry & PDM Network
PO Box 899,
Johnstown, NY 12095

Website

www.pdministry.org

International Phone

518-889-9137
Text: 518-705-1939

INSTRUCTIONS

After reading a chapter in the "Prophets & Prophecy" book, please answer all the questions for that chapter in your workbook. Carefully fill in the blanks, select the correct multiple-choice answer(s) or answer all questions as instructed. Do what you can from memory, and then go back to the book to confirm or complete any answer as needed. Point values for each question are in brackets to the left of the question. Total these points to obtain a final score for each chapter.

For those enrolled in the PDM college course, you must score your workbook and send it in with the final exam request sheet. We will rescore and confirm your workbook scores before we send you a final exam. For PDM students, a passing score on each chapter is 90% or above.

CONTENTS

7 CHAPTER ONE
The Basic Foundation

14 CHAPTER TWO
Prophets and Their Development

23 CHAPTER THREE
The Levels of Prophecy

31 CHAPTER FOUR
The Gifts and Testimony of God to His Church

41 CHAPTER FIVE
Identifying False Prophecy

48 CHAPTER SIX
The Power of a Prophetic Word

53 CHAPTER SEVEN
Prophetic Protocol in the Church

62 CHAPTER EIGHT
Accuracy Verses the Heart of God

68 CHAPTER NINE
Prophetic Operation

78 CHAPTER TEN
Establishing New Prophets

86 CHAPTER ELEVEN
Life as a Prophet

94 FINAL EXAM REQUEST

95 SCORING YOUR WORKBOOK

THE BASIC FOUNDATION

Understanding the foundation for prophets, and the prophetic realm, establishes a solid place to begin. As you go through chapter 1 in this workbook, keep in mind that these basics are the necessary framework for both a healthy walk in God, and a healthy ministry. Unless you are balanced as a person, it is impossible for you to have genuine balance and stability in your ministry. This is the focus of Chapter 1.

. . . .

1. [3] On pages 1-2 of the book the fact that every prophet is still human is

    clearly identified. Prophets have the same _____ but

    they have learned to get _____ over them

    so they don't _____ their lives.

Early Encounters

2. [3] Where in the Bible do we learn about the "five-fold ministry"?

    book: _____   chapter: _____   verse: _____

3. [5] What are the 5 foundational ministries Jesus gave to His Church?

    _____   _____   _____

    _____   _____

4. [5] The office of the _____ has been the most controversial

    and _____ _____ .

    _____ , _____ _____

and _____ _____ have driven the heartiest of souls away from embracing this much-needed biblical ministry.

5. [4] The office of the _____ and the ministry of _____ _____ , with the laying on of _____ , was restored back to the church in the 1940's. This happened in 1948 in Canada through Reg Lazell.

6. [5] Young prophets who don't get taken under someone's wing will spend their early years floundering along, making _____ and _____ for opportunities in hopes that their ministry will find a valid place of _____ .

7. [3] Every young prophet desperately needs to find _____ , instruction, _____ and _____ to become more seasoned and balanced.

8. [3] God-ordained connections, spiritual revelation, soaking in His presence, and personal correction are all important. These things will help to produce not only the kind of _____ you have, but more importantly, the kind of _____ you are.

The Prophetic Realm

Multiple Choice
Select the best answer(s) by circling the letter(s).

9. [2] God uses prophets and their ministry to:

    a. build His people

    b. prophesy only to other Christians

    c. build His Church

    d. give vision and support in times of trouble

    e. all of the above are correct

10. [2] The Hebrew word for "supporting" means:

   a. to establish

   b. to uphold

   c. to strengthen

   d. to build up and refresh

   e. all of the above are correct

11. [5] The ministry of balanced prophets can support, _____ , _____ , and _____ people to _____ _____ in what they have been called to do.

12. [4] There are four important key ideas when it comes to understanding prophets and prophecy. They are:

   a. the _____ of prophets which exist;

   b. the various _____ _____ _____ which operate;

   c. the different types of _____ _____ and how they _____ ;

   d. the kinds of _____ that exist.

Prophets And Their Sphere Of Authority

13. [4] Some prophets are called to function in the local _____ . Others have a ministry that extends out to a given _____ or _____ . Some prophet's minister to entire _____ and others operate on an _____ or _____ level.

14. [3] The Greek word " _____ " is used to identify the

specific _____ _____

_____ any prophet has.

15. [3] The above Greek word applies to anyone who is called to five-fold ministry.

It speaks of the actual _____ , or size of the grasp

or _____ someone has in the _____

and in the natural.

16. [1] Identify where Anna's "metron" was: _____

17. [3] Those trained in a global atmosphere may also assume their ministry is on a

_____ scale. The vast majority of people are called by

God to serve in their _____ _____ .

The ironic thing is, those who do travel internationally end up serving in a

local church anyway when they arrive at their destination. Why? Because

God's heart is for the local Church.

18. [4] When we are _____ _____

and not _____ _____ we

have missed God's heart and that will always cause a huge problem.

19. [2] The _____ of any prophet's ministry is only

limited by the _____ God has placed on it.

20. [3] The Old Testament prophet Jonah was called to a very specific

_____ .

21. [2] What "metron" of prophetic calling did each of the following have?

Moses: _____   Jeremiah: _____

Zephaniah: _____   Agabus: _____

22. [2] Even though God gives the Spirit without measure (metron) to every believer, He _____ where that metron can

_____ .

Multiple Choice
Select the best answer(s) by circling the letter(s)

23. [3] When we step outside our metron:

   a. there is very little difference in our ministry

   b. God honors all our effort and good intentions

   c. the flow of provision will dry up

   d. God's grace just allows us to keep going

   e. none of the above are correct

24. [5] Identify those things that have **no real bearing** on how a prophet actually obtains what God has set in place for them.

   a. driving ambition

   b. personal desire

   c. ability

   d. giftings

   e. all of the above are correct

25. [4] Those who push beyond their actual metron will not have God's

_____ or _____ on them as

they go about trying to _____ their

_____ .

26. [2] God always _____ and _____

people to do the thing He created them to do.

27. [3] Step outside your place of anointing and in that moment the
_____ of God, and the _____ of
God will be gone. Anything you accomplish at this point is by
_____ _____ and
you are operating by _____ ability.

28. [3] When we operate from a place of natural strength and motivation,
the book of James classifies this as _____ ,
_____ and _____ .

29. [3] What is the difference between the gift of teaching and the five-fold
office of the teacher?

_____
_____
_____
_____
_____
_____
_____

30. [2] Every prophet must know their _____
_____ or _____ of authority as
well as the _____ _____ of
_____ they are called.

31. [2] Unhealthy _____ , poor _____
_____ , emotional _____ ,
no submission to _____ , and _____
will bring every prophet to the place of " _____
_____ ". This is the natural belief that success and
anointing in one area _____
_____ them for bigger and better things.

32. [2] The best way to avoid the issue of "terminal misconception" is to

    stay _____ _____ and

    stay _____ _____ .

CHAPTER ONE SCORING

Personal Use *100 Possible Points*	*PDM Use Only* *Certificate of Mastery*
	100 Possible Points

CHAPTER TWO

PROPHETS AND THEIR DEVELOPMENT

In chapter 2 the specific kinds of prophets are examined. Understanding how these ministries are different helps to define what kind of prophet someone may actually be. This chapter also gives a review of how prophets do what they do. The chapter is closed out with a revelatory look at the non-liner nature of God and how that impacts every prophet, and every prophecy that is given.

• •

Basic Kinds Of Prophets

1. [3] Name the three specific types of prophets found in Scripture:

   a. _____   b. _____

   c. _____

2. [4] The great diversity in _____ _____ is based upon what the actual _____ of the prophet is and it relates to the way in which the prophet _____ _____ _____ from God.

3. [3] A genuine seer views their _____ _____ as being a _____ revelation of God's _____ to His people.

4. [3] A seer's clearest, and most accurate revelations always come through this process of _____ , _____ , and _____ .

5. [4] The prophet, who is a seer, predominantly gets what they get by

_____ , _____ _____ ,

_____ God and just being _____

_____ _____ .

6. [2] Experiencing His _____ is the key to life and
revelation for every seer. It is the _____
_____ of their prophetic call.

Multiple Choice
Select the best answer(s) by circling the letter(s).

7. [2] A seer finds their clear prophetic flow by:

   a. direct, immediate, bold action

   b. waiting to be filled with God's heart

   c. soaking in God's presence

   d. deep personal intimacy with God

   e. all of the above are correct

8. [2] In Psalm 27:4 the word "behold" in Hebrew means:

   a. to act with speed

   b. to make bold proclamation

   c. to gaze upon

   d. contemplate with pleasure

   e. none of the above are correct

9. [2] A _____ prophet functions with ease from a
place of _____ , _____ faith.

10. [3] A word prophet often has to learn how to release the
_____ of God with the _____
of God.

11. [2] A word prophet can get a " _____ " of God's

    _____ in the Spirit, and can run with them

    before they ever feel His _____ in the matter.

12. [2] Draw a line through the words on the list below that **do not reflect** the basic
    characteristics that are often found in a "word prophet".

Bold	Highly Relational	Operate From God's Head Verses His Heart
Soaking	Proactive	Operate By Personal Intimacy With God
Raw Faith	Wait In His Presence	Just Fire Off The Word Of The Lord

13. [3] A _____ _____ may function

    like a seer prophet at times and spend a season _____

    _____ _____ . At other times

    they will walk boldly into a situation and just _____

    _____ _____

    _____ _____

    _____ _____ .

14. [2] Every prophet needs to _____ what another prophet

    brings, and learn to _____ and

    _____ them in the way they bring it.

Multiple Choice
Select the best answer(s) by circling the letter(s).

15. [2] To not have a shallow and powerless ministry a prophet must:

   a. seek God

   b. study God's Word

   c. always make sure their voice is heard above others

   d. pray in the Holy Spirit

   e. all of the above are correct

The Place Of Prophets

16. [2] We need to respect ministers before others for what God has _____ them to do. We need to set a good example and _____ _____ to God's servants every chance we get.

17. [2] God alone sets someone in the Body of Christ as a prophet. It will never be the result of _____ _____ , _____ _____ or _____ .

18. [3] The prophet, who is _____ and _____ _____ , will also be _____ in their specific level of prophetic ministry.

How Prophets Opperate

19. [3] Every prophet is nothing more than a _____ _____ or television. They have a God-given capacity to

_____ _____ and receive

_____ _____ _____

_____ _____ . They also have

a _____ from God to _____ what

they receive, when they are told to speak it.

20. [3] The _____ someone has to a prophetic word is nothing

more than a _____ _____ of

their own _____ _____ .

Multiple Choice
Select the best answer(s) by circling the letter(s).

21. [3] When someone has a bad reaction to a genuine prophetic word,
    what is really being exposed is

    a. the prophet must have been wrong.

    b. the person is actually getting angry with God.

    c. the person has personal issues that need to be resolved.

    d. the person may need to make an attitude adjustment.

    e. All of the above are correct.

22. [2] Micaiah demonstrates the _____ every genuine
    prophet must have when _____ with adversity.

Prophets As Time Travelers

23. [3] God views everything from an _____
    " _____ " perspective and can see the beginning and the
    end of our lives as a _____ _____
    _____ _____ . He is

_____ _____ _____

_____ in every event of every life, in every age.

24. [4] God sees your beginning and your end, but not as a

_____ , _____ and

_____ event. For God, your life is a

_____ _____ and any

moment of it can be _____ whenever He wants.

25. [3] A genuine prophet is _____ _____

_____ and " _____

_____ _____ _____ "

with God, when they are prophesying.

The Non-Linear Nature Of God

26. [3] Since God is outside of time He never _____ ,

_____ or _____ any event as if it

moves from _____ to _____ and

into the _____ in a _____ line.

27. [3] People must never assume a prophetic word is _____ in

time when they get it. Nothing in Scripture ever indicates a prophetic word

must be _____ into a linear_____

_____ .

28. [1] In Genesis 46 the _____ _____

God lays out in Jacob's prophecy jumps back and forth over a span of almost

_____ _____ with no indication

that it is doing so.

29. [2] Very few prophets know _____ and _____
God intends to fulfill what He has said.

Multiple Choice
Select the best answer(s) by circling the letter(s).

30. [2] If someone dies before their prophetic word is fulfilled,

    a. the prophet must have missed it.

    b. the person must have been in sin and died before their time.

    c. the prophecy must have been false.

    d. the prophecy could be generational and it will be fulfilled in the future.

    e. none of the above are correct.

31. [2] For anyone called to be a prophet, _____
_____ basically becomes a _____
_____ that puts a _____ right
in the middle of their entire ministry.

Prophetic Bullseye

32. [1] When you receive a genuine prophetic word you become a known
_____ for both _____
and _____ to go after. Heaven targets you to bring
you into a _____ of _____ , hell
targets you to _____ _____
_____ of _____ that
God wants to _____ through you.

33. [1] Genuine prophecy releases a _____
_____ into the spirit realm.

34. [3] The enemy learns for the first time that he has to contend with another

    _____ _____ _____

    on the earth, and that means his forces are being _____

    _____ and thinner with each

    unveiling of _____ .

35. [2] The bigger the _____ between where you are and

    where you are headed, the more _____

    _____ you will have to go through in

    order to get there.

36. [2] Without the required _____ and

    _____ transformation, no prophetic word will ever

    come to pass.

Being A Target

37. [3] Until we are ready to walk in the _____

    _____ , that same word will be the

    _____ of testing in our life. Until we are fit to

    _____ the prophecy the prophecy will continue to

    manifest it's _____ in us.

Multiple Choice. Select the best answer(s) by circling the letter(s).

38. [2] The word "test" in Ps 105:19 means:

    a. to refine gold

    b. to hammer

    c. to shape

    d. smelting in a blast furnace

    e. all of the above are correct

39. [2] No prophet can give you what they _____
_____ . In addition, they can't _____
to you anything unless _____ has specifically
_____ them to do so.

40. [2] It is deadly when your flesh and soul have partial success in false ministry.
Without God's _____ everything you try to do will
eventually _____ _____ .

41. [2] When God so instructs, a prophet can give you what He says, but they can't
give you what they _____ _____ .

CHAPTER TWO SCORING

Personal Use *100 Possible Points*	PDM Use Only *Certificate of Mastery*
[ ]	[ ] *100 Possible Points*

THE LEVELS OF PROPHECY

Chapter 3 introduces the three groupings and six specific levels that all biblical prophecy is broken into. This chapter defines what authority each of the levels have, and how they operate correctly when they are exercised within the specific "metron" that has been established by God.

• •

The Three Prophetic Groups

In the spaces that follow, write in the correct answers.

1. [4] The Three Prophetic Groups Are:

    1. _____
    2. _____
    3. _____

2. [6] The Six Levels Of Prophecy Are:

    1. _____
    2. _____
    3. _____
    4. _____
    5. _____
    6. _____

The Levels Of Prophecy

3. [2] The prophetic realm has different and very _____

_____ of _____ and

_____ .

4. [2] Every _____ expression or _____

activity is not _____ nor is it

_____ .

Level 1 Prophecy

5. [4] The _____ and _____

_____ level of prophecy is _____

_____ _____ _____ .

Multiple Choice. Select the best answer(s) by circling the letter(s).

6. [2] The Greek word for "inspired" found in 2 Timothy 3:16 means:

   a. human breath but it is influenced by God

   b. The "logos" of God breathed into man

   c. breathing in of the breath and life of God

   d. human imagination that is touched by God

   e. none of the above are correct

7. [2] The prophecy of Scripture has the highest level of authority because:

   a. it came by divine inspiration

   b. it is "God breathed"

   c. it is not a result of human thought or ideas

   d. it is the literal "logos" of God that is compiled in the Bible

   e. all of the above are correct

8. [3] God never _____ _____ and

   every _____ _____ will be in

   full agreement with the _____ and

   _____ that is found in Scripture.

True or False. Read the statement below and circle the word "true"
or "false". On the lines that follow defend your answer.

9. [3] Prophecies that are written or spoken today have the same level of authority

   and truth that is found in the Bible.   True   False

Defend Your Answer

_____

_____

_____

_____

_____

_____

_____

_____

_____

_____

_____

_____

Level 2 Prophecy

10. [3] Canonical prophets were under the _____

    _____ of the _____

    _____ as they spoke _____

    and for _____ .

11. [2] What the _____ _____ spoke

    ended up becoming the 66 Books of the _____ .

12. [3] In Scripture a _____ _____
could be a genuine prophet who claimed to speak for God but actually
_____ _____ against Him.

13. [3] When a prophet _____ God's voice they are willfully
_____ with all that is against Him and
that is a very _____ place to be.

Multiple Choice. Select the best answer(s) by circling the letter(s).

14. [2] A New Testament Prophet must

    a. recognize they can be hindered by human error

    b. reveal God's will with accuracy

    c. speak God's word and will with purity

    d. know their God in a deep personal way

    e. all of the above are correct

15. [2] Prophecies that don't agree with Scripture are _____
_____ .

Levels 3, 4 & 5

16. [3] Each part of the Godhead plays a _____
_____ in _____ different
_____ into the Church.

17. [4] The Holy Spirit releases a _____ of
_____ . The word " _____ " is
used here and it means a _____ gift or
_____ _____ .

18. [4] Jesus gave different _____ , which is the Greek word
    " _____ ". This Greek word translates in Scripture as
    _____ , _____ deacons and
    _____ .

19. [5] Ephesians _____ : _____ mentions five specific " _____
    _____ " ministries or _____ .
    These five are: _____ _____
    _____ _____
    _____

20. [5] God the Father releases _____ of
    " _____ ." This is the Greek word
    " _____ " and it speaks of something that is
    _____ _____
    _____ within someone.

21. [4] The "operation" God the Father placed within each person might be called
    the " _____ _____
    _____ " since it literally is the _____
    that the " _____ " of God has on us as
    _____ .

22. [2] When we don't do things the way God _____ them for
    us, we become nothing more than a _____
    _____ .

23. [5] Until the _____ , _____ and
    _____ He placed in us find their
    _____ _____ , we will all operate
    at a much _____ _____ than
    God intended.

24. [1] "You were born an _____ , don't die a

_____ ."

Old & New Testament Prophets

25. [4] Old Testament prophets were the only _____ of God

authorized to _____ _____

_____ .

Provide The Information

26. [10] In the spaces below, identify the five specifics given in Scripture to identify true prophecy and false prophets in the Old Testament.

a. _____

_____

_____

_____

Scripture: _____

b. _____

_____

_____

_____

Scripture: _____

c. _____

_____

_____

_____

Scripture: _____

d. _____

_____

_____

_____

Scripture: _____

e. _____

_____

_____

_____

Scripture: _____

True or False (Note: Please read Galatians 2:1-2 to answer question 27.)
Circle "true" or " false". On the lines that follow defend your answer.

27. [4] According to Gal.2:1-2, five-fold ministers need to be submitted under valid biblical authority.   True   False

Defend Your Answer

_____

_____

_____

_____

_____

_____

_____

_____

_____

_____

In Your Own Words

28. [6] Explain what Paul did in Gal.2:1-2 and why his actions and revelation apply to every legitimate five-fold minister who wants to biblically fulfill their call in God.

_____

_____

_____

_____

_____

_____

_____

_____

_____

_____

_____

_____

_____

_____

_____

CHAPTER THREE SCORING

Personal Use *100 Possible Points*	*PDM Use Only* *Certificate of Mastery*
	100 Possible Points

THE GIFTS AND TESTIMONY OF GOD TO HIS CHURCH

In chapter 4 an introduction is given to prophetic levels 3,4,5 and 6. How these levels differ and what the demonic counterpart looks like are also reviewed. In addition the proper use of the gifts is explained in order to bring some clarity on when and how they should be used in a church service.

• •

Level #3 – The Office Of The Prophet

1. [2] New Testament _____ do make

   _____ and God's Word has a _____

   for this very thing.

2. [2] In 1 Thes. 5:19-20 we are instructed; "do not quench the Spirit, do not despise

   prophetic utterances. But _____ everything carefully;

   _____ _____ to that which is

   good". (NASB)

Multiple Choice
Select the best answer(s) by circling the letter(s).

3. [2] 1 Thes. 5:19-20 implies that there will be prophesies spoken that will **not**

   be good. Circle the letters that explain what to do with these.

a. hold on to it just in case some part of it could be correct

b. throw out the word and the one who gave it

c. copy it down and save it as an example of a bad word

d. throw the word out

e. none of the above are correct

4. [2] A prophetic word that is **not** recorded or written down, but is left to memory,

a. remains pure and will be of great value for years to come.

b. will usually be recalled with great accuracy and detail.

c. is valid and should be highly valued.

d. is basically worthless, gets mixed up in the mind of the one who heard it.

e. none of the above are correct

Safeguards In Prophetic Ministry

5. [2] Any prophecy you _____ must be spoken by someone who has the _____ and the _____ to do so.

6. [3] A well intentioned Saint who gives you a word in private, apart from the Church leadership is out of God's _____ . This kind of _____ is a _____ _____ of pastoral _____ .

7. [3] You must consider the _____ life of the one doing the prophesying. People with _____ ministry, _____ instability, or _____ character have the potential of _____ a _____ _____ in those who listen to them.

Prophetic Ministry Check List

Place an "X" in the box of those items that are on the prophetic ministry checklist.

8. [3] [ ] Is the local leadership present when the word is spoken?

   [ ] Do they have validation by other proven prophets?

   [ ] Do they have a profound, accurate gift ?

   [ ] Will you remember the word with clarity and accuracy?

   [ ] Is the person emotionally and spiritually sound?

   [ ] Did they know clear details that only God could have told them?

   [ ] Are they submitted under valid biblical authority?

   [ ] Do they have proven good character?

   [ ] Have they ever ministered at a well know prophecy conference?

Level 4 – The Gift Of Prophecy

9. [2] According to 1 Cor. 14:3 in the KJV Bible, the gift of prophecy has three clear functions. They are _____ , _____ and _____ .

Multiple Choice
Select the best answer(s) by circling the letter(s).

10. [2] The gift of prophecy

   a. can provide direction and correction if no prophet is present

   b. brings genuine edification and true comfort to those in need

   c. can at times be used to strongly rebuke those in sin

   d. can bring exhortation to those who need it

   e. all of the above are correct

When Prophecy Is Not Prophecy

11. [2] Just because something is _____ does not

    mean it is a _____ .

12. [3] The gifts operate at different _____ based

    upon our _____ of them and the level of our

    _____ .

13. [3] When a gift is _____ it should always be for the

    _____ _____ _____

    _____ , not for personal _____ .

Gifts In The Church Service

Multiple Choice
Select the best answer(s) by circling the letter(s).

14. [2] During service, when you feel God stirring or speaking within,
    you should

    a. wait until you know what God is doing at that moment in the service

    b. jump right up and do something in order to obey the Holy Spirit

    c. speak out loudly at that moment because you don't want to miss God

    d. say or do anything that comes to mind so you don't grieve the Holy Spirit

    e. none of the above are correct

15. [2] The distinct possibilities of how you **should respond** when you feel God
    moving in a service are:

    a. speak out immediately in a loud voice the moment you feel God moving

    b. wait to see if God is speaking personally to you

    c. wait to see if you just understand what He is doing with the whole church

    d. speak out because God wants you to explain what His is doing

    e. all of the above are correct

16. [2] From a biblical perspective this means _____ out of _____ times when our gifts are stirred in service it requires us to _____ or _____ nothing.

A Demonic Counter Part

17. [3] God placed in every human a _____ _____ with specific _____ . These will help them most effectively do what they were _____ to do.

Multiple Choice
Select the best answer(s) by circling the letter(s).

18. [2] When satan fell his gifts

   a. were eliminated and stopped functioning

   b. fell with him

   c. began to operate from a dark, ungodly place

   d. were no longer very powerful and could not be used by man

   e. none of the above are correct

19. [2] Gifts cry out to function the way God created them. This is why the unsaved

   a. will usually plug into God and be used by Him in amazing ways

   b. will plug into an ungodly spiritual source to still use their gifts

   c. can have their spiritual gifts hijacked by a demonic source

   d. can operate as a counterfeit to the real thing

   e. none of the above are correct

PROPHETS & *Prophecy*

Relationship & Revelation Vs. Knowledge & Information

20. [8] Satan and his demons are not _____ or

_____ . They are not an _____

_____ to God and do not know

_____ that is going on. They have no

_____ of God's Word and have no

_____ about the _____ .

Multiple Choice. Select the best answer(s) by circling the letter(s).

21. [2] Psychics are deceiving to unsuspecting people because

    a. they actually here from God and are speak the truth

    b. they may have a spiritual gift but it's plugged into a demonic source

    c. they have no gift at all and just get lucky in what they say

    d. there is a supernatural element to what they do

    e. none of the above are correct

True or False
Answer the statement below by circling "true" or "false".
Defend your answer on the lines that follow.

22. [5] A psychic operates by genuine revelation because what they say may actually be something the person does not know.   True   False

_____

_____

_____

_____

_____

_____

23. [2] Those who want the supernatural but _____

_____ will still get power but it will be a

_____ .

Level 5 – The Grace Gift Of Prophecy

24. [2] The Greek word "energema" used in 1 cor. 12:6 relates to what the Father gives. This comes from a root word that means:

_____

_____

_____

25. [2] Romans 12 says the _____ _____

function best in the parameters set in place for them by

_____ .

26. [8] Identify the grace gifts as they are listed in Romans 12.

a. _____

b. _____

c. _____

d. _____

e. _____

f. _____

g. _____

h. _____

Multiple Choice
Select the best answer(s) by circling the letter(s).

27. [2] The prophetic grace gift

     a. views everything as black and white

     b. provides clear direction in confusing situations

     c. sees life from the viewpoint of uncertainty

     d. can make good decisions when others are not sure what to do

     e. all of the above are correct

28. [2] The weakness of those who have a prophetic grace gift in operation can be

     a. impatience with others who need more time to make decisions

     b. irritation with those who need all the facts before moving ahead

     c. impulsiveness that upsets others by quickly making decisions

     d. making decisions with little or no planning

     e. all of the above are correct

Level 6 – The Spirit Of Prophecy

29. [4] The _____ of prophecy may fall on a congregation when there is a high level of _____ and _____ . When this happens the spirit of prophecy will _____ _____ to _____ when they may never have spoken out before.

30. [5] In essence, the _____ _____ _____ is the testimony of _____ as He speaks through _____ about what He is doing or _____ for His _____ at that moment.

31.   [2] The Spirit of Prophecy may come upon _____
_____ or whole _____ .

Aspects Of The Spirit Of Prophecy

32. [4] Our _____ _____ has
a prophetic _____ because it is also the
_____ , the true record of what
_____ has done for us, in our life. Our
_____ is _____ that
the enemy cannot change.

33. [2] Giving an " _____ " testimony will
_____ the Spirit and He will not
_____ our _____ .

Multiple Choice. Select the best answer(s) by circling the letter(s).

34. [2] A good presentation of your testimony should

    a. be very graphic, last an hour or more and cover every detail of your life

    b. be from the heart, genuine and honest

    c. speak about what happened the day you met Jesus and how you changed

    d. focus mainly on you and cover nearly all the sins you ever committed

    e. all of the above are correct

35. [4] "The season of life you are in will determine what core nature of God will manifest." Use the lines below to explain what this statement means.

_____
_____
_____
_____
_____
_____
_____
_____
_____
_____

CHAPTER ONE SCORING

Personal Use 100 Possible Points	*PDM Use Only* *Certificate of Mastery*
	100 Possible Points

IDENTIFYING FALSE PROPHECY

Chapter 5 takes a closer look at the different aspects of prophecy and what is at the core of false prophecy. It exposes and removes many of the misguided teachings that have been promoted over the years. In addition it explains what happens when a genuine prophet speaks and what happens when a prophet "misses it".

• •

Multiple Choice
Select the best answer(s) by circling the letter(s).

1. [2] When a genuine prophet speaks a prophecy into the atmosphere

    a. their voice aligns on earth with what is being spoken in heaven

    b. nothing really happens because only God speaks with creative power

    c. it is a partnership between the prophet, the prophecy and God

    d. it is as if God is the one speaking and that word is fully released into its purpose to do the job it was sent to do

    e. all of the above are correct

2. [4] The _____ of creation moves from the _____ of God and gives _____ to the existence and _____ of man.

3. [3] What Samuel _____ actually became the _____ _____ God used to shape the _____ and _____ of the nation.

41

4. [3] The genuine _____ of God is always

   _____ in _____ prophecy.

5. [6] Once a prophet _____ from God and

   _____ His word out into the _____ ,

   things begin to happen. The _____ life of God is a

   living, _____ and powerful

   _____ that begins to _____

   _____ _____ _____ .

How False Prophecy Happens

Multiple Choice
Select the best answer(s) by circling the letter(s).

6. [2] Every valid prophetic utterance

   a. will line up with the Scripture

   b. will have the "Logos" or life of God in it

   c. will have God's heart attitude woven through it

   d. will sound important and be spoken with great enthusiasm

   e. all of the above are correct

7. [2] False prophecy

   a. can come from a prophets natural mind or visual cues

   b. can come from a wrong heart attitude

   c. always sounds strange and is very easy to recognize all the time

   d. can come from a prophet who has a fleshly or emotionally messed up life

   e. all of the above are correct

8. [8] When prophecy is only built around _____ and
_____ use of the gift, things are going to
_____ _____ ... All too often,
someone's zeal to use a newly _____
_____ is nothing more than a _____
for their own _____ _____
_____ and _____ ego.

True or False

*Read the statement below and respond by circling "true" or
"false". On the lines that follow defend you answer.*

9. [10] Believing and following a "missed" word is really no big deal. God's grace
will just cover the mistake and there's nothing to worry about.
True   False

Defend Your Answer

_____
_____
_____
_____
_____
_____

10. [7] "Parking lot prophecy" is a powerful way to develop and expand your
ministry and be recognized as a genuine prophet.
True   False

Defend Your Answer

_____
_____
_____
_____
_____
_____

Multiple Choice
Select the best answer(s) by circling the letter(s).

11. [2] If a false word is believed and acted upon

    a. God has to deal in new ways with that person to get them back on track

    b. the person moves away from where they should be going

    c. God has to begin purging away the mess that resulted from that word

    d. the person will experience trials that could have been avoided

    e. all of the above are correct

12. [2] The danger when someone speaks as if it's God, when it's not, is that

    a. it points people in the wrong direction

    b. people spend time, energy and resources on something God will not bless

    c. people can become bitter and discouraged when it does not come to pass

    d. someone's true calling in life can be delayed or even lost

    e. none of the above are correct

When There Is No Anointing

13. [6] The _____ _____ assigned to you only know _____ _____ _____ . That means they have _____ _____ if a word you are given is _____ .

14. [6] Isaiah 10:27 makes it very clear that the _____ in your life is what _____ _____ _____ . When you are _____ for something you are not _____ to do there is no _____ . You are stuck _____ something that was never supposed to be your _____ .

Multiple Choice
Select the best answer(s) by circling the letter(s).

15. [2] Receiving prophetic ministry from just any source that comes along

    a. can become a very spiritually dangers thing to do

    b. can become a very emotionally frustrating thing

    c. is something you should seek out every chance you get

    d. can make you vulnerable to unwarranted attacks from the enemy

    e. all of the above are correct

16. [2] A prophetic word can be technically accurate but still be a false prophecy

    a. because the prophet got information from God's head not revelation from God's heart

    b. because the prophet spoke what God said but did not feel what God felt

    c. because the prophetic word was delivered at the wrong time

    d. because the prophet misrepresented the heart of God when he spoke

    e. all of the above are correct

17. [5] When it comes to a false _____ speaking a false _____ into your life, don't _____ it. If you do, and embrace what was said you have given _____ _____ an open _____ to mess with your _____ .

The Two Kinds Of Prophecy

18. [6] On the lines below identify the two kinds of prophecy found in Scripture:

    a. _____

    b. _____

True or False. Read the statement and circle "true" or false".
On the lines that follow defend your answer.

19. [10] Prophecy that falls under God's prophetic will is absolute because God's will always happens.   True   False

Defend Your Answer

_____

_____

_____

_____

_____

_____

_____

_____

_____

_____

Multiple Choice
Select the best answer(s) and circle the letter(s).

20. [2] What items below are examples of God's **prophetic plan?**
    a. the birth of the Messiah

    b. Israel leaving Egypt in Exodus

    c. Moses prophesying that he would lead Israel to the promised Land

    d. the abomination of desolation spoken of by Daniel and Jesus

    e. all of the above

In Your Own Words
Read the statement that follows and answer the question on the lines provided.

21. [10] Jesus said *"it is the will of the Father that none should perish"* in Matthew 18:14, yet we all know that people die, perish and go to hell every day. Why is Jesus still **not** a false prophet, even though what He said does not come to pass for millions? Explain your answer on the following lines.

_____
_____
_____
_____
_____
_____
_____
_____
_____
_____
_____
_____
_____
_____
_____
_____
_____
_____
_____

CHAPTER FIVE SCORING

Personal Use *100 Possible Points*	*PDM Use Only* *Certificate of Mastery*
	100 Possible Points

THE POWER OF A PROPHETIC WORD

I n Chapters 6 of the book, several important issues are covered. First of all there is a candid look at the need for prophets to be submitted under authority. They don't' have universal permission to prophesy over the sheep as they wish. Secondly is the need for prophets to develop godly character and emotional and spiritual maturity so they don't destroy their own ministry or mess up those they minister to.

· ·

1. [10] If the _____ is messed up, if they have no

    _____ _____ and don't have the

    _____ of God, then the _____

    they release will be a _____ _____

    up _____ as well.

Multiple Choice
Select the best answer(s) and circle the letter(s).

2. [4] When a prophet releases a true prophetic word prematurely

    a. it can cause a problem for the recipient

    b. the person will not be properly equipped to walk in it successfully

    c. it will frustrate the one it was intended for

    d. it's no big deal and the person can just move right ahead with it

    e. all of the above are correct

3. [4] To deliver a prophetic word in proper biblical order a prophet must have what two things? (circle two only)

   a. a clear prophetic gift even if they are not submitted under anyone

   b. permission to deliver that word from the person's oversight

   c. a record of accurate prophetic words in the past

   d. authority to release the word because they are in their "metron"

   e. all of the above are correct

True or False
Circle "true" or "false" to indicate your answer.

4. [4] Prophets can speak over anyone they want because they have universal authority over God's people.   True   False

5. [4] Prophets must submit under the pastoral oversight of those they are ministering to.   True   False

6. [4] The mess that is within a prophet's character is not a problem as long as they have a very clear and accurate prophetic word.   True   False

7. [4] Unresolved personal and emotional issues in a prophet's life will filter how they hear and deliver every prophetic work they give.
   True   False

8. [6] Every prophet who really wants to _____
   _____ for the better must _____
   _____ for their own _____
   _____ first.

9. [5] The _____ inside the prophet is going to be
   _____ a piece at a time with _____
   _____ they deliver.

Multiple Choice
Select the best answer(s) and circle the letter(s).

10. [4] A prophet with an unrefined character is dangerous because they

    a. actually sow mixed seed into the lives of those they prophesy over

    b. will create confusion in those they prophesy over

    c. will deposit unhealthy things along with the prophetic word

    d. may choke out the seed that really is good within the person

    e. all of the above are correct

11. [15] When prophets impart _____ _____ _____ into good soil, _____ _____ will spring up. However, when prophets sow _____ _____ into good soil a mixed _____ mess will thrive and that will produce an _____ and _____ harvest.

The Impact Of Prophecy

True or False
Circle "true" or "false" to indicate your answer.

12. [4] There is great impact on the heart, mind and spirit of the one who receives a genuine prophetic word.   True   False

13. [4] There is no problem with receiving a prophetic word from one who has a remarkable gift but has a clear lack of character development.
True   False

14. [4] As a messenger of God, every prophet has the authority to say whatever they want regardless of their heart condition or the situation.   True   False

15. [4] What comes out of a prophet's mouth will always benefit the people no matter what or how it is said, because the prophet speaks for God.
True   False

The Ten Tests Of Prophecy

16. [10] Circle the letter of the following are **not** part of the ten tests of prophecy.

a. is the prophet under authority and in their "metron"?

b. does the prophetic word make you feel excited and fire you up?

c. does the prophecy contradict Scripture in any way?

d. is the prophecy delivered in a clear, understandable way?

e. is the prophet well known?

f. is the life or "Logos" of God evident in the prophetic word spoken?

g. does the word promote you and your ministry?

h. was your leadership present or in agreement with the ministry?

17. [10] On the lines that follow explain why churches often don't have a good balance when it comes to prophets and prophetic ministry.

_____
_____
_____
_____
_____
_____
_____
_____
_____
_____
_____

CHAPTER SIX SCORING 6

Personal Use
100 Possible Points

PDM Use Only
Certificate of Mastery

100 Possible Points

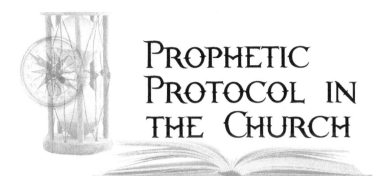

PROPHETIC PROTOCOL IN THE CHURCH

In this chapter the safeguards God put in place for how prophets should judge each other is addressed. These key ideas help prophetic ministry work in prophetic teams and fit properly into the local church. It also explains why every prophet must submit under the leadership of the local church where they are called to minister.

• •

Read over 1 Cor. 14:29-33 and 37-38 to answer the following questions.

1. [5] When two or three prophets prophesy in a service, who is to pass judgment on what was said?

    Answer: _____

Explain your answer:

_____
_____
_____
_____
_____
_____

2. [2] Who is the **"all"** that is being referred to where the Apostle Paul wrote "for you can *__all__* prophesy"?

    Answer: _____

3. [5] Explain on the lines below why 1 Cor. 14:29-33 is **NOT** a proof text when it comes to the whole congregation thinking they can all prophesy?

_____

_____

_____

_____

_____

_____

4. [5] Paul wrote *"if a revelation is made to another (prophet) who is seated, let the* first (prophet) keep silent. For you (the prophets) can all prophesy one by one….".* (Parentheticals added by the author to bring clarity) Why it is so important for prophets to "give honor" to one another by allowing each another to speak, when working in teams of two or three, as is common in "prophetic presbytery"? Explain your answer on the lines that follow.

_____

_____

_____

_____

_____

_____

_____

_____

_____

_____

_____

_____

_____

_____

_____

_____

5. [5] 1 Cor. 14:32 refers to the prophets human spirit, not the Holy Spirit when it says; *"The spirits of prophets are subject to prophets".* In light of this scripture explain why prophets must allow God to refine their natural tendencies when it comes to their delivery of a genuine prophetic word.

_____

_____

_____

_____

_____

_____

6. [5] If odd behavior is not proof of the Holy Spirit moving on someone, why do so many people feel they have to do something strange when they minister or move in one of the gifts?

_____

_____

_____

_____

_____

_____

7. [5] Explain why King James English is not wrong, it's just not necessary when a person operates in any of the vocal gifts or especially when prophesying.

_____

_____

_____

_____

_____

_____

8. [5] Even under God's _____ , when speaking God's word, a prophet is still _____ _____ _____ . For the most part they don't become some strange acting, _____ - _____ , totally _____ person.

9. [5] If a prophet is _____ , _____ and _____ in life these _____ will often show up in their _____ _____ as well.

Multiple Choice
Select the best answer(s) and circle the letter(s).

10. [2] Identify the tendencies **that can be harmful** to a prophet's ministry. Circle the letter(s) of the best answer(s).

    a. continually unnecessary odd behavior

    b. clear delivery and tenderness of heart

    c. unrestrained, unrefined natural tendencies

    d. being abrupt, impatient or never getting to the point

    e. all of the above are correct

11. [5] The capacity of a prophet to _____ in the Spirit and release their ministry is there because it is what _____ _____ them to do. It is their _____ _____ _____ and automatically _____ out of them.

12. [8] On the lines that follow, identify the foundations stones of a world class prophetic ministry.

    a. _____

    b. _____

    c. _____

    d. _____

    e. _____

    f. _____

Releasing Prophetic Ministry

Multiple Choice

Select the best answer(s) and circle the letter(s).

13. [2] Seasoned prophets know;

    a. they are not dependent on a momentary rush of the Holy Spirit

    b. their office, place in God and ministry is like a river that gushes forth

    c. they can and should prophesy over anyone, any place, anytime

    d. they don't always speak everything that God may show them

    e. none of the above are correct

14. [5] On the lines below explain why the "grab and blab" pattern of flowing in the gifts can be so destructive.

    _____

    _____

    _____

    _____

    _____

    _____

How Prophets Function

Multiple Choice
Select the best answer(s) and circle the letter(s).

15. [2] Circle the letter(s) of the analogy(s) that represent what prophets do, or how they operate when they are ministering to God's people.

   a. they are a hammer that smashes anything they don't like

   b. they are a pipeline between God and man

   c. they are a conduit through which God speaks to people

   d. they are a spiritual blueprint reader that speaks what God wants to build

   e. all of the above

16. [2] Each time or _____ ordained by God had a _____ prophet that spoke for what God was doing.

17. [3] Prophets do not know _____ about every _____ , _____ or season. They only know what God _____ _____ and can only speak what He _____ them to say.

Multiple Choice
Select the best answer(s) and circle the letter(s).

18. [2] Genuine prophecy

   a. is never considered to be an absolute certainty

   b. is a divine possibility

   c. is a partnership between God, the prophet and the person who got it

   d. is dependent on how well the person cooperates with God to obtain it

   e. all of the above are correct

19. [2] A valid prophetic word will be fulfilled

    a. no matter what the person does

    b. even if the person refuses to change or mature in any way

    c. when the person really tries to make it happen

    d. even if the person will not position themselves to obtain the promise

    e. none of the above are correct

20. [2] The great killer of great words is

    a. human nature

    b. unrefined character

    c. delay and natural thinking

    d. refusal to change

    e. all of the above are correct

21. [2] Our life-long job is to see to it that our _____ does not direct the outcome of our _____

    _____ .

The Prophet's Reward

22. [4] On the lines that follow explain what the prophet's reward is.

    _____

    _____

    _____

    _____

    _____

    _____

23. [4] The reward a prophet _____ into you as they minister depends more on _____ _____ _____ _____ and the _____ of their _____ , than it does on the _____ of what they are saying. As a result, the _____ that is left behind can either be _____ or _____ , and few people understand this important principle.

24. [5] The _____ a prophet broadcasts of themselves may not be _____ _____ _____ _____ . Impartation comes from the _____ of _____ , not the _____ of it. A prophet who looks good on the outside but is _____ _____ on the inside will mess up the one who _____ _____ _____ from them.

25. [2] Select the letter(s) of those **unhealthy traits** a genuine prophet could display and yet still be able to speak clear, precise accurate prophetic words.

    a. wrong behavior or unrefined character

    b. immaturity both spiritual and emotional

    c. open or hidden sin

    d. rudeness or lacking tenderness of heart

    e. all of the above

True or False

Read each statement below and circle true or false to indicate your answer.

26. [2] The ability to operate in the gifts is proof that someone has a pure heart and good character.   True   False

27. [2] God desires people to get their eyes off the gifts and ministers and place their devotion back on Him.   True   False

28. [2] Good character and rich personal relationship with God are important. However, moving profoundly in the gifts and having a great ability to speak are the real keys that identify a prophet's ministry.   True   False

CHAPTER SEVEN SCORING

Personal Use *100 Possible Points*	*PDM Use Only* *Certificate of Mastery*
	100 Possible Points

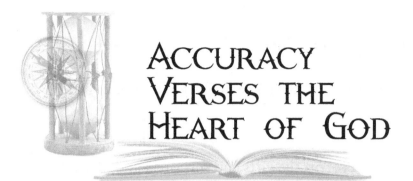

ACCURACY VERSES THE HEART OF GOD

In Chapter 8 of the book, the issue of prophetic accuracy is address as it relates to the heart of God. The fact that a prophet can be very accurate is actually a secondary issue. When it comes to valid prophetic ministry, the greatest question that needs to be addressed is whether the prophet actually had God's heart, or only spoke God's mind when they released the prophetic word.

• •

Multiple Choice

Select the best answer(s) and circle the letter(s).

1. [5] Matthew 7:22-23 a key verse when it comes to understanding any kind of ministry from God's point of view. Circle the letter(s) of the correct statement(s).

   a. we can use the gifts and not really intimately know the "Giver" of them.

   b. spiritual activity does not automatically mean God accepts it as valid.

   c. we can do the work of God and not have the heart of God while doing it.

   d. unless the life of God is imparted, the work of God has not happened.

   e. all of the above are correct

2. [5] The Greek word for know is "gnosis" and it means

      a. to be able to use a spiritual gift with power

      b. a firsthand knowledge of

      c. to be teachable

      d. an intimate knowledge of

      e. all of the above

3. [4] Using a spiritual gift without being in intimate relationship with God is

      a. fine as long as the gift is accurate and used correctly

      b. a normal practice that God accepts

      c. a form of spiritual prostitution

      d. impossible because the gifts don't operate that way

      e. none of the above are correct

4. [10] Prophetic ministry that is built on _____ _____ will not produce anything of _____ _____ . It will not meet with_____ _____ and those who function this way are ultimately going to be identified as those who "_____ _____".

Multiple Choice
Select the best answer(s) and circle the letter(s).

5. [5] The *"argos rhema"* that is mentioned in Matthew 12:36 means

      a. technically accurate and full of God's life and power

      b. powerless even though it is technically accurate

      c. true but still empty and void of the Spirit and life of God

      d. not accurate but still filled with God's power and life

      e. none of the above are correct

6. [5] True prophecy is

    a. only based upon how accurate a word is

    b. about releasing something from the heart of God

    c. released through anyone who can hear God's voice

    d. released by those who correctly represent the one who sent them

    e. all of the above are correct

7. [5] In Exodus 17:6 Moses preformed a mighty miracle and the people drank and were blessed. However, in Numbers 20:1-2 Moses preformed the exact same miracle yet this time his actions brought the discipline of God which ended his ministry and prevented him from entering the promised land. **Circle the letter of the statement(s) that identify why this happened.**

    a. his frustration with the people caused him to disobey God.

    b. he displayed anger that misrepresented the heart of God.

    c. he struck the rock and did not speak to it.

    d. he broke an Old Testament "type".

    e. all of the above are correct

True or False

Read the statement and circle True or False. On the lines that follow defend your answer.

8. [12] The ministry mistakes of an immature or unrefined prophet are not really a problem because God covers our mistakes.   True   False

Defend Your Answer

_____

_____

_____

_____

_____

_____

_____
_____
_____
_____

9. [12] Misrepresenting God is not that big a deal for a prophet.   True   False

Defend Your Answer

_____
_____
_____
_____
_____
_____
_____
_____
_____
_____

10. [12] God spends a great deal of time working on the character, heart and mind of those who are called to be genuine prophets.   True   False

Defend Your Answer

_____
_____
_____
_____
_____
_____
_____
_____
_____

_____

_____

_____

_____

_____

_____

_____

_____

_____

11. [15] Having a tender heart is not that important when a prophet is delivering a prophetic word to one of God's sheep.   True   False

Defend Your Answer

_____

_____

_____

_____

_____

_____

_____

_____

_____

_____

_____

_____

_____

_____

_____

_____

_____

12. [10] Explain the significance of the following statement from the bottom of page 155 in the book, "Prophets & Prophecy":

"Until a prophet grasps the significance of knowing God's heart in what is said, they will never be able to really know and release God's will to His people"

_____

_____

_____

_____

_____

_____

_____

_____

_____

_____

_____

_____

_____

_____

_____

_____

CHAPTER EIGHT SCORING

Personal Use 100 Possible Points	PDM Use Only Certificate of Mastery
	100 Possible Points

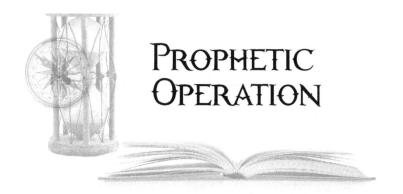

Prophetic Operation

I n Chapter 9 of the book, the different styles of prophecy and the different kind's of prophetic meetings are looked at. In this overview, prophetic presbytery, open meetings, ordination and chamber prophecy are all examined. We discover that each has its own function and specific purpose as designed by God for His church.

• •

The Prophetic Presbytery Meeting

Multiple Choice

Select the best answer(s) by circling the letter(s).

1. [2] Prophetic Presbytery was reintroduced to the Church in
    a. 1957 through Oral Roberts
    b. 1906 through William Seymour
    c. 1948 through Reg Lazell
    d. 1985 through Rick Joiner
    e. none of the above are correct

2. [2] Today people can expect to receive Prophetic Presbytery
    a. only once in their lifetime
    b. once or twice a year
    c. whenever they want it
    d. several times during their lifetime
    e. all of the above are correct

3. [2] Prophets in a prophetic presbytery team

    a. work together in tandem

    b. can impart spiritual gifts

    c. speak words that can be used to do strong spiritual warfare

    d. must be suited to this specific kind of prophetic ministry

    e. none of the above

4. [5] When a true prophecy is released to someone by a _____ _____ team the _____ will come to steal, _____ and _____ that word. ... Each person will have to _____

_____ _____

_____ _____

_____ _____ to see it come to pass.

The Prophetic Presbytery Team

True or False

Read the statement and circle True or False.

5. [2] Anyone who wants it can call in a Prophetic Presbytery team.
    True   False

6. [2] Prophetic Presbytery is general prophecy that is spoken over anyone present in a meeting. It really is not very useful to church leadership.
    True   False

7. [2] Prophetic Presbytery serves to set people into the foundation of the local church. It helps identify specific ministries and brings order.
    True   False

8. [4] A prophetic presbytery team works spiritually in a _____
_____ _____ to establish,
_____ and _____ the members
of a church into their _____ .

Receiving Prophetic Presbytery

Multiple Choice

Select the best answer(s) and circle the letter(s).

9. [2] Those receiving the ministry of prophetic presbytery

   a. are picked at random by the prophets during the meeting

   b. are in need of more direction, conformation or clarification of ministry

   c. must receive instruction about what to expect from the ministry

   d. don't have to be part of that specific local church

   e. all of the above are correct

10. [2] The prophetic presbytery team

   a. is made up of any 5 fold ministers that can work well together

   b. must be able to release clear, balance prophetic words

   c. must flow as one and honor each other

   d. must have ministry styles that complement and enhance each other

   e. all of the above are correct

11. [2] A prophetic presbytery team comes to

   a. read the spiritual blueprint of those who are committed to that church

   b. clarify personal callings

   c. confirm ministries

   d. identify areas that are a strength or that may need change

   e. all of the above are correct

12. [10] On the lines below describe what the basic format is for how a "prophetic presbytery" meeting is conducted.

_____

_____

_____

_____

_____

_____

_____

_____

_____

_____

Multiple Choice
Select the best answer(s) and circle the letter(s).

13. [2] Preselected people being brought forward is call a "_____"

    a. calling

    b. grouping

    c. gathering

    d. setting

    e. none of the above are correct

14. [2] The prophecies over those receiving ministry

    a. are brief and to the point

    b. are 5 to 8 minutes in length

    c. are very general and non-specific in mature

    d. are 20 to 30 minutes in length

    e. none of the above are correct

Who Should Get The Ministry

True or False

Read the statement and circle True or False. On the lines that follow defend your answer.

15. [10] Prophetic Presbytery can be given to anyone, even visitors.

    True   False

The Open Meeting

16. [5] Place an "x" on the items that define the basic concepts of an open meeting.

    [ ] a. It usually begins with a time of worship.

    [ ] b. Preselected people are set before the church to receive ministry.

    [ ] c. People are "called out" of the general congregation to receive ministry.

    [ ] d. The word is usually preached before any ministry is done.

    [ ] e. The kind of ministry done is generally less specific than presbytery.

    [ ] f. This is a great place for a life calling or new ministry to be identified.

    [ ] g. Lengthy, detailed specific words are expected in this kind of setting.

    [ ] h. Visitors get ministered to even though their leaders are not present.

17. [3] No prophet has the authority or right to randomly place _____

_____ into the sheep of _____

_____ . They must have permission from the person's

_____ _____ to do so.

18. [3] Prophets who put prophetic " _____ " into another's

sheep without the oversight's agreement have _____ that

_____ _____ . In addition they

have _____ the _____ that sheep

has with their shepherd.

19. [4] Put an "x" on the items that define the concept of ***"illegitimate ministry"***

[ ] a. birthed with the knowledge and agreement of the person's leadership

[ ] b. conceived outside of the church family from a questionable source

[ ] c. dishonors the church leadership and church vision

[ ] d. is supported by and submitted to the church leadership

[ ] e. is prophesied by an unknown source and moved upon anyway

[ ] f. is not confirmed or embraced by the church leadership

[ ] g. operates independently of the person's church and leadership

[ ] h. flows well with the church vision and recognizes church authority

A Second Type Of Open Meeting

20. [5] Explain how it works if another prophet is given the opportunity to speak at a meeting when they are **not** the invited guest speaker. Who are they really submitted under and who has the final authority in that meeting?

_____

_____

_____

_____

_____

_____

_____

_____

_____

_____

Ordination

21. [2] Ordination is usually the _____

    _____ that marks the beginning of someone's

    _____ _____ and

    _____ into five-fold ministry.

22. [2] A _____ _____ officially

    recognizes the personal call on someone without _____

    them on their own.

23. [3] Until an individual has _____ themselves

    _____ to their calling and faithful to their

    _____ , they are not ready to be

    _____ _____ on their own.

    Only _____ and _____ prove

    a ministry.

Multiple Choice
Select the best answer(s) and circle the letter(s).

24. [2] The actual biblical standard for ordination is

    a. a good college education

    b. lasting fruit

    c. faithfulness to ministry and leadership

    d. have a genuine calling to a specific ministry

    e. all of the above are correct

Chamber Prophecy

25. [6] On the lines below identify the two kinds of "chamber prophecy".

    a. _____

    _____

    _____

    b. _____

    _____

    _____

26. [4] Place an "x" in the box of all those that apply to the following statement: Conference prophecy can be

    [ ] a. the most dangerous and untested kind of prophecy to receive

    [ ] b. the experimental use of spiritual gifts by unstable people

    [ ] c. useful if it is recorded and reviewed by your church leadership

    [ ] d. given by those who have lives full of rebellion and sin

    [ ] e. very specific and used to redirect your life calling and future ministry

    [ ] f. done by those who have only had a minimal level of training

    [ ] g. a huge problem if the person's pastor has no idea what was spoken

    [ ] h. a valid and powerful tool you can always trust in your spiritual life

True or False
Read the statement and circle true or false. Defend your answer on the lines that follow.

27. [4] Conference prophecy is a good place to get direction for your life calling, specific ministry and personal vision.   True   False

Defend Your Answer

_____

_____

_____

_____

_____

_____

_____

_____

_____

Multiple Choice
Select the best answer(s) and circle the letter(s).

28. [2] Conference prophecy

    a. is on equal ground with a word spoken by a seasoned prophet

    b. is as safe as a word given in prophetic presbytery

    c. can always be used to do spiritual warfare

    d. does not need to be recorded or review by anyone in leadership

    e. none of the above are correct

29. [2] Conference prophecy

    a. can be beneficial to bring confirmation

    b. can be an encouragement to new believers

    c. can be used to train people in the use of spiritual gifts

    d. can be used to help people hear the voice of God

    e. all of the above are correct

30. [2] Those who receive conference prophecy

    a. must be aware of the dangers it presents

    b. can relax and have no need for concern about what is spoken

    c. know that everyone speaking over them is well qualified and pure

    d. should realize there is no way to know who is speaking into their life

    e. none of the above are correct

CHAPTER NINE SCORING

Personal Use 100 Possible Points	PDM Use Only Certificate of Mastery
	100 Possible Points

ESTABLISHING NEW PROPHETS

In Chapter 10 of the book, the need for raising up the next generation of prophetic ministry is addressed. How that is done, and what the guidelines are that may help in the process are all reviewed in detail. Also, the misuse of the word "prophetic" is reviewed and how to identify genuine prophets is covered in some detail.

• •

1. [5] On the lines below explain what can happen to a young prophet that does not get the proper mentoring by seasoned prophets.

_____

_____

_____

_____

_____

_____

2. [3] Place an "x" in the box next to the items that define what the "Elisha" form of mentoring involves.

[ ] a. Go to the mentors meeting to receive guided instruction

[ ] b. Be part of the ministry team and participated in everything that goes on

[ ] c. Be in meetings to sit alongside and get under the mentors anointing

[ ] d. Be in meetings to direct what happens and speak with power

[ ] e. Speak at the mentors meeting when invited and if it is appropriate

[ ] f. Be in a place to take over in case the mentor makes a mistake

[ ] g. Look at an invitation to attend a meeting as an endorsement of ministry

Simple Guidelines For An "Elisha"

True or False

Read the statement and circle true or false.

3. [2] A prophet has the right, once an "Elisha" is identified, to invite them attend a meeting, no matter what their pastor says.   True   False

4. [2] Notify every church that an "Elisha" will be joining you for ministry.
    True   False

5. [2] Let the "Elisha" do whatever they want during the meeting.
    True   False

6. [2] The "Elisha" will split any offering with the prophetic mentor.
    True   False

7. [2] Set aside a specific time to evaluate how the "Elisha" did.   True   False

8. [2] There is no need to go over anything with the pastor since they are not a prophet and will not understand what went on.   True   False

The Dark Side Of Prophecy

9. [10] On the lines below explain how prophecy can be used in the wrong way.

_____

_____

_____

_____

_____

_____

_____
_____
_____
_____
_____
_____
_____
_____
_____
_____
_____

Multiple Choice
Select the best answer(s) and circle the letter(s).

10. [2] At times a valid prophetic word can be pulled out

    a. and used wrongly to shake people up

    b. and specific portions of it can be used to direct things a certain way

    c. of context to make it say something it does not

    d. as a last resort to control what people do

    e. all of the above

11. [2] What you are called to do does not _____ _____ or become _____ because you may have changed your church. God gave you that _____ and it will _____ _____ in your life.

12. [2] Prophecy unfolds due to the _____ of your

_____ and your _____ to serve
God. It is not so much a result of the _____
_____ of your body.

13. [3] When a valid prophetic word is spoken over your life, the
_____ of that word has more _____
than the _____ of where it was spoken.

14. [3] The _____ in God's mind is always
_____ and _____ than
just one moment or one location.

Place an "x" in the box next to each statement that is correct.

15. [4] When it comes to prophecies, if your church ever closes down

[ ] a. your prophetic words cannot come to pass.

[ ] b. your ministry can still find it's expression elsewhere.

[ ] c. your life has been wasted and basically thrown away.

[ ] d. your ministry can never be fulfilled.

[ ] e. Your ministry has not ended because that church is gone.

[ ] f. You have to receive other prophecies since these are no longer valid.

16. [4] When it comes to God's will, and attending a local church

[ ] a. it is very narrow and once you mess up, your spiritual life is destroyed.

[ ] b. no church is really God's will for your life and any church will do.

[ ] c. you may have to find another place if things become unhealthy.

[ ] d. if you are not being fed or feel unsafe, you can find another church.

[ ] e. no matter what, you must stay put even if you feel like you are dying.

[ ] f. you can go elsewhere the moment you disagree or feel uncomfortable.

[ ] g. if you like the music and programs that must be God's will.

17. [4] A prophetic word used incorrectly

 [ ] a. can become a shackle to hold someone in place.

 [ ] b. can be pieced together from different sources to make a point.

 [ ] c. can be used to create fear in people.

 [ ] d. can cause guilt.

 [ ] e. is not something that can actually happen in a church setting.

 [ ] f. may bring about a spirit of control.

 [ ] g. is only going to be a problem in religious cults.

18. [4] If a prophetic word is being used incorrectly on you, you should

 [ ] a. accept it and trust the leadership no matter what happens.

 [ ] b. graciously walk away from that leadership and church.

 [ ] c. argue and become critical of those leaders and that church.

 [ ] d. move on and find a new church where you can grow.

 [ ] e. defend your position and stay there no matter how it hurts you.

 [ ] f. find a church where you can be encouraged and healed up.

 [ ] g. honestly express your concerns with the oversight of the church.

True or False
Circle "true" of "false" to indicate your answer to each statement.

19. [2] A prophetic word being used to usurp a pastors authority is fine because a real prophecy has more authority than the pastor.   True   False

20. [2] When the dark side of prophecy shows up it is usually because people have their own idea of how that word is to be used.   True   False

21. [2] The dark side of prophecy is just a simple mistake and when it happens no harm is really done.   True   False

Identifying Genuine Prophets

22. [3] Every activity of the _____ _____ now seems to have the word " _____ " attached to it, and that has created _____ of the _____ . Thus prophetic intercession, prophetic worship. prophetic evangelism and a host of other things are simply spirit led and have been incorrectly labeled as "prophetic".

23. [3] The best worship is always _____ _____ but that does not mean it is biblically correct to call it _____ _____ .

Place an "x" in the box to indicate the correct answer(s).

24. [4] Automatically adding the word "prophet" to our dreams, our worship and our intercession

    [ ] a. is not biblically correct

    [ ] b. is a common mistake people make

    [ ] c. is a good idea because it lets people know how spiritual we really are

    [ ] d. has added a lot of confusion when it comes to what really is prophetic

    [ ] e. is something we need to honestly look at and in some cases stop doing

25. [4] 98% of the "prophetic conferences" that go on

    [ ] a. are not prophetic at all

    [ ] b. are really just places for gift activation and experimentation

    [ ] c. have people attending that for the most part are not prophets

    [ ] d. have very little prophetic revelation being released

    [ ] e. teach about the power and use of gifts which is not prophetic

Characteristics Of Genuine Prophets

True or False

Circle "true" or "false" to indicate your response to each of the statements.

26. [2] Prophets don't need to filter their ministry through the gifts or inner promptings. They have a direct connection with God and operate in their ministry from that place of pure flow.   True   False

27. [2] Prophets have the secret counsel of God revealed to them.   True   False

28. [2] Genuine prophets speak to the future   True   False

29. [2] Genuine prophets have direct profound encounters with God   True   False

30. [2] Genuine prophets have the past revealed to them in unique ways.
                                                                    True   False

31. [2] Genuine prophets carry an anointing that impacts others.   True   False

32. [2] Genuine prophets speak in generalities that could mean anything.
      True   False

33. [6] On the lines that follow explain why the teaching of a prophet can be very different from the teaching of others.

_____

_____

_____

_____

_____

_____

_____

_____

_____

_____

_____
_____
_____
_____
_____
_____

CHAPTER TEN SCORING

Personal Use
100 Possible Points

PDM Use Only
Certificate of Mastery

100 Possible Points

LIFE AS A PROPHET

In the final chapter of the book, what life is like for those called to be prophets is examined. How a prophet's ministry may develop over time is also reviewed. Finally, what the impact is of genuine prophecy is looked at in some detail.

• •

1. [5] Scripture instructs us to _____

_____ _____

_____ and   He will drew near to you. Your

_____ is to discover how to _____

_____ _____

_____ and stay there. That _____

you correctly to _____ _____

_____ , know His _____ and

_____ _____ from

the Holy Spirit.

2. [10] A genuine prophetic ministry will develop over time and in specific stages. It also has strong spiritual challenges to overcome. Below is a list of what happened in the life of prophet Emmons as he grew in his calling. Place these in the correct order using numbers to indicate what happened first(1), what happened second(2) ... etc....

_____ saw a river flowing from left to right

_____ heard a mocking demonic voice

_____ saw black and white pictures or what looked like
          video clips

_____ got spontaneous songs

_____ saw colored objects that had symbolic meanings

_____ had a unique activation of the gift of tongues

_____ spoke a pure unfiltered word that came right out
          of his spirit

_____ throw a bucket into the river and look in it

_____ led worship seminars and led conference worship

_____ a portal opened up in the spirit realm

Place an "x" in the box of every true statement that is listed below

3. [2] [ ] A prophet has no need for physical promptings or emotional hooks to
    release a genuine prophecy.

4. [2] [ ] A prophet is not dependent on natural cues to release a spiritual reality.

5. [2] [ ] Prophets must always see or feel something before they can prophesy.

6. [2] [ ] Our natural body is designed by God to be aware of the spirit realm.

7. [2] [ ] Our soul is conscious of our emotional and intellectual state.

8. [2] [ ] Our spirit is in direct contact with the Holy Spirit.

9. [2] [ ] Prophets function exactly like those who flow in spiritual gifts.

10. [2] [ ] Prophets must be willing to be an unconscious conduit for God.

11. [8] On the lines that follow explain what "power evangelism" is and why it was so effective in the restaurant that was mentioned in Ch. 11 of the book.

_____

_____

_____

_____

_____

_____

_____

_____

_____

_____

_____

_____

_____

_____

_____

12. [8] Prophet Emmons sites several examples where he was allowed to see and communicate with those who had gone on to be with the Lord. In the Gospels Jesus was on the Mount of Transfiguration with his disciples and He also spoke with those who had departed the earth many years earlier. Both of these are **<u>not a violation</u>** of God's law that clearly forbids anyone from speaking with the dead? However, in I Samuel 28:14 Saul speaks with Samuel who had died, and the judgment of God fell on him, Explain the difference.

_____

_____

_____

_____

_____

_____

_____

_____

_____

_____

_____

_____

_____

_____

13. [8] Based upon what happened with the prophetic word given to Lance Wallnau by Prophet Emmons, explain why the validity of a prophecy is not to be determined by how long or how well polished the delivery of that word is.

_____

_____

_____

_____

_____

_____

_____

_____

_____

_____

_____

_____

_____

14. [4] The moment a prophet begins to _____

    _____ about what is being _____

    they will be ruled by _____ _____ and

    their ministry is basically over.

15. [4]15. As a prophet I have to _____ the fact that life with

    God is an _____ . There are constant

    _____ and continual _____ that

    I am presented with and must adjust to.

Prophecy Made A Difference

16. [8] Explain the impact and importance when God drew prophet Emmons back
    in time about an hour in order to minister over the couple in Albany, NY.
    (Page 203 in the text.)

_____

_____

_____

_____

_____

_____

_____

_____

_____

_____

_____

_____

_____

Basic Principles

17. [8] Place an "x" on the line(s) that identify the basic principles that must flow in a prophet's life in order for them to fulfill their ministry.

   [ ] a. they must ignore correction and reject those who don't believe

   [ ] b. they must stay hungry and stay close to God

   [ ] c. they must be willing to take risks and try the impossible

   [ ] d. they must never make a mistake

   [ ] e. they must never try anything unless they are sure it will not fail

   [ ] f. they must not let criticism discourage them

   [ ] g. they must be willing to look foolish at times

18. [2] What two qualities keep a prophet's ministry pure and acceptable to God?

   a. _____

   b. _____

19. [3] If you are called as a prophet then you should _____
   _____ and continue to _____ into
   the _____ _____ of
   _____ you have been given.

Multiple Choice
Select the best answer(s) and circle the letter(s).

20. [2] The simple keys that unlock every ministry are

   a. hunger after God

   b. don't let failure or intimidation be an option

   c. try several times and then know when it's time to quit

   d. accept and learn to love correction

   e. promote yourself and your ministry when it is appropriate

   f. all of the above are correct

21. [2] To develop their ministry a prophet should

    a. question everything and not trust anyone

    b. get up beside those who know more than they do

    c. study the Word and pray in tongues

    d. force themselves on mature ministry and show up where ever they go

    e. listen to the teachings and the heart of mature prophets

    f. none of the above are correct

22. [4] The ability and _____ any prophet has will always be developed through a _____ - _____ walk of _____ and faith. We are all a

_____ _____

_____ and our ability to _____

_____ continues to unfold from year to year so we can

_____ _____

_____ His people.

Place an "x" in the box that makes the statement true.

23. [4]23. When it comes to establishing a successful ministry you will have to

    [ ] a. fight your way to the top and guard that position.

    [ ] b. embrace the fact that you are going to make mistakes.

    [ ] c. understand that mistakes can be used by the enemy to define you.

    [ ] d. remember that the Holy Spirit can use mistake to refine you.

    [ ] e. know that people are a key that will bring you to the people, places, truths and vision you will need to be known and successful.

    [ ] f. let God bring the divine alignments and connections of your destiny

    [ ] g. remember to grab every opportunity you can to move forward.

True or False

Circle "true" or "false" to indicate your response to each of the statements.

24. [2] A deeper, more intimate relationship with the Lord will help to develop a prophet's ministry and calling.　　　　　True　　False

25. [2] If a prophet stays alert and grabs every opportunity they can to be seen and heard, this will bring the alignments and connections they need to grow their ministry bigger and faster.　　　　　True　　False

26. [2] Praying in tongues, learning to move by the Spirit, entering into worship, studying Scripture and embracing discipline are the major things God uses to bring every prophet into their full calling.　　True　　False

CHAPTER ELEVEN SCORING

Personal Use 100 Possible Points	PDM Use Only Certificate of Mastery
	100 Possible Points

Final Exam Request

"I am enrolled in the PDM Network "Prophets & Prophecy" course. By signing my name below I am requesting to take the final exam in order to receive a "Certificate Of Mastery" from the PDM Network. I attest to the following things:

1. I am enrolled in the "Prophets & Prophecy" course and I have read and studied the book "Prophets & Prophecy", by Prophet William Emmons;

2. I have completed the companion workbook and passed every chapter with a score of 90% or above;

3. I am sending this final exam request page along with my workbook for PDM to rescore. If PDM agrees that I have passed each chapter with 90% or above they will send me a final exam. I have two weeks from the day I receive the exam to complete it and mail it back to PDM. They will score my exam and notify me of my grade;

4. 4. If my final exam score is below 80% I do have the right to take the "second chance" final exam after rereading the book and redoing the workbook. I will submit a $20 exam processing fee if I choose to take this second exam. If I do not get a passing grade on the second exam I will not be issued a "Certificate Of Mastery" for this course.

(Please Print Below)

I _____ sign my name below, having met the above conditions. I request to take the final exam and if I pass it with a score of 80% or above , I desire to be issued a "Certificate Of Mastery" from the PDM Network. If I do not meet the minimum score requirement I understand I do have the right to apply for the "Second Chance" final exam.

Signature: _____ *Date:* _____

Mailing Address: _____

City: _____ *State:* _____ *Zip:* _____

Email: _____ *Mobile #:* _____

<table>
<tr><td>**PDM Use Only**
1st Exam Score</td><td>**PDM Use Only**
2nd Exam Score</td></tr>
</table>

Comments:　　　　　　　　　　　**Certificate Issued:** ☐ **YES** ☐ **NO**

Scoring Your Workbook

If you are self-scoring your workbook and not taking the course through the PDM Network, you will now go back and check your answers against the book text. Answers that are incorrect must be marked as wrong and then corrected as needed. Please score this workbook with care and honesty. Keep in mind that you must have a score of 90% or above on every chapter to have achieved a passing grade on the material. Once you are finished scoring add up the points missed and then deduct that total from 100. This is your final score for that particular chapter. Your final average can be found by totaling all your final scores and then dividing by 11.

If you are taking this as a class through the PDM network, please mail the scored/corrected workbook and the exam application to our home office. This allows you to take the final exam and receive a certificate of mastery when your final exam is passed with a minimum score of 80%.

Only those enrolled through the PDM network should fill out the final exam application and mail it, and their workbook, to us for secondary scoring. This permits us to verify your scores and send you the final exam to obtain a certificate of mastery through our network. If you are taking this as a class in a Bible school setting your instructor will provide you with correct instructions at this point.

Once you receive the final exam from PDM, you have two (2) weeks to complete it and then mail it back to our home office for scoring.

<u>During the exam you cannot look back to the author's book for any answers.</u> You can however keep your Bible handy and use it as a reference source as needed.

After PDM scores your exam you will be informed if you have passed the course or not. Those who pass will be issued a certificate of mastery and we will mail the certificate, your workbook and your exam back to you.

If you fail the exam we will return it and your workbook back to you. If you so desire, you will have one more opportunity to take a "second chance" final exam. We suggest you re-read the book and re-do the workbook before you apply for the secondary final exam. To apply, please mail your workbook, the exam application and a $20 check or money order to our home office address.

If you are successful in passing the second chance final exam, we will issue you a certificate of mastery and mail it, your exam and your workbook back to you. If you are not successful in passing this exam, no certificate can be issued to you for this course. We will however, mail the exam and your workbook back to you.

Prophet William Emmons

www.pdministry,org
PropheticDestinyMinistry@gmail.com

Made in the USA
Middletown, DE
04 March 2023

26180978R00057